ISBN 978-0-260-56466-5
PIBN 11120851

KETING SUGAR BEETS

NOVEMBER 1956
AMS No. 137

ATES DEPARTMENT OF AGRICULTURE
Marketing Service
Research Division

ngton

CONTENTS

SUMMARY

This is a report on a brief study of the contracts and possible alternative methods of pricing beets. It sets forth and analyzes certain basic questions confronting growers who might wish to change the present contracts under which the growers and processors sell and buy beets.

Grower-processor contracts throughout the beet sugar industry rest basically on one principle: A sharing of the net return from sugar sales by the grower and the processor. The division is made somewhat differently in the areas east and west of the Mississippi River. This report deals primarily with practices in the western areas.

Several alternate price bases were found to be statistically feasible. To avoid having the factory management in sole control of merchandising expenditures, payments to growers could be made on the basis of the average net return for all factories in the western regions, rather than the net return to the individual factory. To avoid the use of net return at all, the basis of payment might be made the gross return, either for the factory or for all western factories. It would be possible to get entirely away from returns for beet sugar as a basis, by adjusting to a national average sugar price--for raw sugar, wholesale refined sugar, or retail refined sugar.

In form, these adjustments would seem to avoid one or another problem in the basis for beet payments. In average effect, however, such statistical adjustments would not appreciably change prices paid to growers.

The only assurance of any substantial adjustment in the division of the returns from sugar sales must be through the bargaining between growers and processors. This bargaining would determine the price at which grower and processor are willing, and economically able, to commit their beets and their services to the enterprise and to carry their share of the marketing risks.

Sugar production has been encouraged in the United States from earliest times. In the last quarter of the nineteenth century, the first successful beet sugar factories were established in California and Michigan. Now roughly a quarter of the sugar consumption in the country comes from mainland sources. Three-fourths to four-fifths of this domestic production is beet sugar, the remainder being cane sugar.

Sugar beets are grown in scattered areas in the Lake States, on the northern Great Plains, and westward to the Pacific Coast. In recent years, there has been some shift of sugar beet production westward and, at the same time, some development of marketing problems for beet sugar. In western growers' associations, a question has arisen whether the marketing problems might be alleviated by certain changes in the grower-processor contracts under which beets are sold to the factories.

MARKETING SUGAR BEETS

By Donald Jackson, D. B. DeLoach, and Rado J. Kinzhuber*
agricultural economists, Marketing Research Division
Agricultural Marketing Service

PRICING SUGAR BEETS

The problem presented here concerns basically the distribution (sharing) of the consumer's dollar paid for sugar. It should be considered in light of the setting outlined in the latter part of this report. Both the quantitative division and the principle, or method, by which division is made require examination.

Underlying the immediate problem of the sharing of the consumer's dollar paid for sugar are the changes taking place in the production of beets and the customary practices of marketing sugar. Beet production has shifted westward since World War II. The industry growth has been particularly noticeable in the West Coast States and Idaho where beet culture appears to enjoy a relatively favorable cost-price position compared to other crops and other producing areas. This growth of western beet production caused a rise in beet sugar available for sale in consumption markets outside the far west where the major part of the output had been sold.

In order to sell western beet sugar in the States east of the Rocky Mountains the western processor had to meet the price competition from midwest beet sugar processors and from the cane sugar refineries on the Atlantic, Gulf and California coasts. They incurred heavier transportation and marketing cost which began to affect adversely the net return on sugar and the resulting payment to beet growers who have contracted annually to share all marketing costs prior to calculating their final price for beets. The lower net returns to beet growers resulting from higher marketing costs are strictly in line with the customary western contract between the growers and processors. However, as net returns decline there are two features of the existing contracts that have begun to bother growers. The first is that the contract gives the processor complete control over the marketing process, the costs of which are deductable from the gross selling price for sugar, the second is an impression that the contract basis for sharing marketing costs between the grower and processor encourages processors to indulge in excessive marketing expenditures. For these reasons, representatives of western sugar beet growers' associations have requested that the basis of their grower-processor contracts be reviewed and any feasible alternative methods be pointed out.

* Rado J. Kinzhuber transferred to the Grain Division of Commodity Stabilization Service before the study was completed.

Since 1952, the costs of marketing beet sugar appear to have in-
eased sharply for factories in some areas, and there is considerable
eling in the industry that the difficulties of marketing also have
creased; that is, that competition has become keener. In addition
the feeling of increasing economic pressure on the industry, some
et growers' groups have felt their contracts with processors made
em vulnerable to bearing too much of the increases in costs of mar-
ing. The principal increase in marketing difficulties appears,
never, to be the trend toward increasing marketing costs.

Total per capita sugar marketings have been practically constant
ing the past 20 years. Furthermore, the 40 percent increase in
et sugar marketings over the 20-year period represented a small net
n in percentage of the total United States sugar supply. Since
ld War II, the beet sugar supply has just about held even, on the
erage, with other sugar supplies.

One purpose of the quota-and-allocation system is to avoid the
essure of oversupplies on the market that might require increased
keting effort and cost. Also, sugar price trends suggest peculiar
keting difficulties. Compared with average prices during the period
7-49, wholesale granulated sugar prices advanced 9 percent to 1954,
1 7 percent from 1947 to 1955. In the same periods, processed foods
a group advanced 5 percent and 2 percent, respectively.

Data are not available to indicate whether beet sugar processors,
order to hold their share of the market, incurred relatively higher
keting costs than other sugar processors, or higher costs than food
cessors as a group.

The dissatisfaction of many western growers over prices they re-
ived for sugar beets from the 1954 and 1955 crops has centered on
increased cost of marketing the sugar produced from their beets.
never, there is a definite relationship between the increased mar-
ing cost caused by selling sugar in more distant and competitive
kets and the increased production of sugar beets and beet sugar on
Pacific Coast.

If sugar marketing costs had remained unchanged, there might have
eloped an extremely favorable competitive position for Pacific Coast
t growers. Beet marketing costs have risen, however, and dissatis-
tion has resulted.

One basic type of grower-processor contract is in use throughout
sugar beet regions. The important uniform feature is the statement
a basis on which to divide the net proceeds from the sale of sugar
the coming season, rather than a statement of a fixed price to be
id for sugar beets. The method of division differs between the East
l the West. In the East, the net proceeds from sugar sales for a
ason are commonly divided evenly between processors and growers. In
West, however, a more complex scheme is employed under which pay-
ts vary with quality of beets, and payments for any one quality of
ts vary with the average of the season's net proceeds per pound of
gar sold.

The contract normally states the acreage of beets that a grower will produce and deliver, the services that the processor will furnish to the grower, the supervision he will have over cultural methods, harvesting time and methods, and the time and conditions of delivery. It shows the scale of prices which the grower will receive for beets of various sugar contents, at various levels of average net return per 100 pounds at which the season's sugar may be sold.

The following paragraphs and the scale table of sugar beet prices give an illustration of the typical western sugar beet contract (table 1).

The table of beet prices, representing changes in the "sliding scale" of payments for varying quality of beets and varying net sugar proceeds, differs to a minor degree between areas and between factories, but the logic it represents is the same in all the contracts.

The price per ton of beets delivered is determined by the average net return per 100 pounds of sugar sold by the processing company and the average percent of sugar in the beets, whether individual test or factory or district average sugar content is used.

The actual amount of net derived from each ton of beets depends also on the percentage of sugar content that is extracted from the beets. At 86 percent efficiency of extraction, approximately the average for the industry, the factory obtains only 86 percent of the sugar in the beets, but the producer is paid on the basis of the total sugar content, regardless of the efficiency of extraction. Not only does the producer receive the stipulated amount from each 100 pounds of sugar sold by the factory, but also he receives a like amount for each potential 100 pounds of sugar that the factory did not extract. Table 2 shows the processor's share of net returns per ton from sale of sugar for which grower payments are shown in table 1. According to table 1, a grower delivering beets with 15 percent sugar content would receive $10.47 per ton of beets when the net return 1/ for the factory or settlement area averaged $7 per 100 pounds of sugar. Total net per ton on sugar from the same beets at 86 percent efficiency of extraction would be $18.06.

Figure 1 shows the grower's payments for beets with 15 percent sugar content as percentages of total net received at a factory with 86 percent efficiency. At $3 net return per 100 pounds of sugar sold, the grower receives about 42 percent of the net return. With increases in net return, the grower's share rises until at $7.50 the grower is receiving 59 percent of net returns, whereas the processor's share is 41 percent. The division then remains about the same until $9 in net return is reached.

1/ The "net return" as basis for payment for beets is determined by deducting from the gross sales price of sugar sold all sales and marketing expenses, such as freight charges on sugar, loading and handling charges, sales department salaries, advertising, brokerage, and commissions.

Table 1.—Typical schedule of processor's payments to grower per ton of beets, western area, 1955

Average net return per 100 pounds of sugar in beets	Percentage sugar in beets											
	23	22	21	20	19	18	17	16	15	14	13	12
Dollars	----Dollars----											
9.00	21.57	20.57	19.57	18.58	17.59	16.61	15.64	14.67	13.71	12.75	11.80	10.86
8.50	20.42	19.47	18.52	17.58	16.64	15.71	14.79	13.87	12.96	12.05	11.15	10.26
8.00	19.27	18.37	17.47	16.58	15.69	14.81	13.94	13.07	12.21	11.35	10.50	9.66
7.50	18.12	17.27	16.42	15.58	14.74	13.81	13.09	12.27	11.46	10.65	9.85	9.06
7.00	16.61	15.82	15.04	14.26	13.49	12.73	11.97	11.22	10.47	9.73	9.00	8.27
6.50	15.09	14.37	13.65	12.94	12.24	11.54	10.85	10.16	9.48	8.81	8.14	7.48
6.00	13.57	12.91	12.26	11.62	10.98	10.35	9.72	9.10	8.49	7.88	7.28	6.68
5.50	12.05	11.46	10.88	10.30	9.73	9.16	8.60	8.05	7.50	6.96	6.42	5.89
5.00	10.53	10.01	9.49	8.98	8.47	7.97	7.48	6.99	6.51	6.03	5.56	5.10
4.50	9.02	8.56	8.11	7.66	7.22	6.79	6.36	5.94	5.52	5.11	4.71	4.31
4.00	7.87	7.46	7.06	6.66	6.27	5.89	5.51	5.14	4.77	4.41	4.06	3.71
3.50	6.72	6.36	6.01	5.66	5.32	4.99	4.66	4.34	4.02	3.71	3.41	3.11
3.00	5.57	5.26	4.96	4.66	4.37	4.09	3.81	3.54	3.27	3.01	2.76	2.51

Table 2.--Sugar beet processor's share in "net return" per ton of beets, plant extraction efficiency f 86 percent

Average net return per 100 pounds of sugar in beets	Percentage of sugar in beets											
	23	22	21	20	19	18	17	16	15	14	13	12
Dollars	----------Dollars----------											
9.00	14.03	13.49	12.93	12.38	11.82	11.25	10.68	10.10	9.51	8.92	8.32	7.72
8.50	13.21	12.69	12.18	11.66	11.14	10.61	10.06	9.52	8.87	8.42	7.85	7.28
8.00	12.38	11.90	11.43	10.94	10.45	9.96	9.45	8.95	8.43	7.91	7.39	6.85
7.50	11.55	1.1	10.67	10.22	9.77	9.31	8.84	8.37	7.89	7.41	6.92	6.42
7.00	11.08	10.67	10.24	9.82	9.39	8.94	8.50	8.04	7.59	7.13	6.65	6.18
6.50	10.62	10.23	9.83	9.42	9.00	8.58	8.15	7.73	7.29	6.84	6.39	5.94
6.00	10.17	9.79	9.41	9.02	8.63	8.23	7.82	7.41	6.99	6.57	6.14	5.70
5.50	9.71	9.35	8.99	8.62	8.24	7.87	7.48	7.09	6.69	6.28	5.88	5.46
5.00	9.25	8.91	8.57	8.22	7.87	7.51	7.14	6.77	6.39	6.01	5.62	5.22
4.50	8.78	8.47	8.14	7.82	7.49	7.14	6.80	6.44	6.09	5.73	5.35	4.98
4.00	7.95	7.68	7.39	7.10	6.80	6.49	6.19	5.87	5.55	5.22	4.88	4.55
3.50	7.13	6.88	6.63	6.38	6.12	5.85	5.57	5.29	5.01	4.72	4.42	4.11
3.00	6.30	6.09	5.88	5.66	5.43	5.20	4.96	4.72	4.47	4.21	3.94	3.68

TOTAL SUGAR DELIVERIES 1/

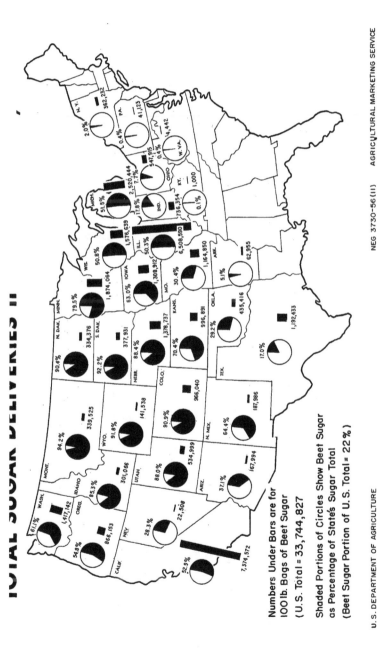

Numbers Under Bars are for
100 lb. Bags of Beet Sugar
(U.S. Total = 33,744,827

Shaded Portions of Circles Show Beet Sugar
as Percentage of State's Sugar Total
(Beet Sugar Portion of U.S. Total = 22 %)

U. S. DEPARTMENT OF AGRICULTURE

NEG 3730-56(11)   AGRICULTURAL MARKETING SERVICE

Figure 1

Many beet growers are represented as satisfied with the structure and price gradations given by the sliding scale, if net proceeds from sugar sales are to be the basis of payments. They are said to object to the principle of basing payments on net proceeds. The central objection to the use of net proceeds as a basis of payment, however, applies to some extent to any alternative basis that rests on the division of the coming season's proceeds from sugar sales. The objection is that the processor, in carrying out the merchandising of the sugar, has complete control and discretion in making expenditures; yet these expenditures are all deducted from gross proceeds in arriving at the net proceeds that are to be divided between processor and grower.

If the processor should, within his marketing quota, unwisely produce more sugar than he could sell economically, and incur heavy marketing costs to sell it, the grower would suffer. Indeed, he would suffer disproportionately, because of the "sliding scale" provision in his contract whereby, when the net return from sugar is relatively low, the producer receives a lower percentage of the net than when net return is relatively high. Thus the fluctuation in net receipts from sugar sales is exaggerated in the growers' beet payments.

Normally, the grower's share in the income from beet sugar sales is reduced, when there is an increase in merchandising costs, by an amount varying from 50 percent to 60 percent or more of the merchandising cost increase. The amount of the deduction depends on (1) quality of beets, (2) the amount of the net proceeds, and (3) the particular variation of the sliding scale used.

Alternative bases suggested which retain the income-sharing feature include: National average raw sugar price, a similar wholesale refined sugar price, a similar retail sugar price, gross returns from beet sugar sales (either local or national), and, as a partial alternative, national average net returns from beet sugar sales (table 3).

Use of national average net returns would make the least disturbance in present methods of computing payments (figure 2). The same sliding scale might be used except where the growers and processor recognized that a factory stood competitively above or below the national level. In such instances, every price figure on the scale table would need to be adjusted by the relationship between local and national net returns.

A certain amount of stability of payment would be achieved because year-to-year changes in a national average are certain to be less than those in the items that make up that average. Use of the average would practically preclude the influence that increases in a processor's merchandising expenditures could have on growers' payments under the current system. In any given year, such a change in basis might be advantageous to growers in one area and to the processor in another.

Table 3.--National average sugar prices and returns on sales of beet
sugar by sugar factories, annual, 1935-1955

Year	:	Sugar prices per 100 lbs.			:	Returns for beet sugar		
	:	Raw	Refined		:			
	:		Wholesale	Retail	:	Gross	:	Net
	:	Dollars	Dollars	Dollars		Dollars		Dollars
1935.........	:	3.23	5.85	5.7				4.05
1936.........	:	3.61	4.69	5.6				4.25
1937.........	:	3.45	4.74	5.6				3.69
1938.........	:	2.94	4.48	5.3				3.29
1939.........	:	2.99	4.57	5.4				3.28
1940.........	:	2.79	4.34	5.2				3.58
1941.........	:	3.37	4.91	5.7				4.32
1942.........	:	3.74	5.44	6.8				4.52
1943.........	:	3.74	5.49	6.8				4.58
1944.........	:	3.74	5.46	6.7				4.67
1945.........	:	3.75	5.39	6.7				5.05
1946.........	:	4.61	6.34	7.7				7.13
1947.........	:	6.22	8.12	9.7				6.48
1948.........	:	5.55	7.61	9.4		8.411		6.61
1949.........	:	5.81	7.81	9.5		8.455		6.69
1950.........	:	5.93	7.84	9.8		8.727		6.96
1951.........	:	6.06	8.21	10.1		9.100		7.27
1952.........	:	6.26	8.45	10.3		9.369		7.46
1953.........	:	6.29	8.55	10.6		9.044		7.14
1954.........	:	6.09	8.55	10.5		8.851		7.00
1955 1/......	:	5.95	8.42	10.4		--		--

1/ Preliminary.

Source: USDA, Commodity Stabilization Service, Sugar Division.

Use of a processor's gross proceeds from sugar sales, instead of
net, as a basis of growers' payments would require an adjustment between the normal levels of gross and net. Data available indicate
that, as an average in recent years, net has run very close to 80 percent of gross, 20 percent of gross having gone into merchandising
charges. Application of gross returns to beet payments in these terms
would require the lowering of each figure on the scale table by 20
percent, to keep current payments on their present level. Control of
merchandising costs by the processors would still have its effect on
growers' payments, but in a manner different from the present. A
processor might have two potential sales of sugar in sight, one at a
higher price and higher merchandising cost, the other at lower price
and lower cost. Competitive self-interest would then dictate to him
that he seek the higher price of the two only if the difference in

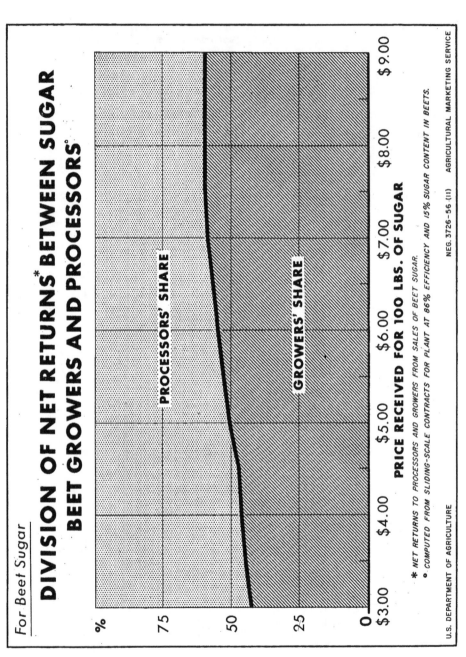

For Beet Sugar

DIVISION OF NET RETURNS* BETWEEN SUGAR BEET GROWERS AND PROCESSORS°

PROCESSORS' SHARE

GROWERS' SHARE

%

75

50

25

0

$3.00 $4.00 $5.00 $6.00 $7.00 $8.00 $9.00

PRICE RECEIVED FOR 100 LBS. OF SUGAR

* NET RETURNS TO PROCESSORS AND GROWERS FROM SALES OF BEET SUGAR.
° COMPUTED FROM SLIDING-SCALE CONTRACTS FOR PLANT AT 86% EFFICIENCY AND 15% SUGAR CONTENT IN BEETS.

U.S. DEPARTMENT OF AGRICULTURE   NEG. 3726-56 (11)   AGRICULTURAL MARKETING SERVICE

Figure 2

gross left him a margin above the difference in cost. There could be
no assurance that the beet grower's share of gross returns would ex-
ceed his share of net returns. Conversion of the basis to gross
returns could have a significant effect on the geographical distribution of beet sugar.

With gross returns, as with net, the use of a national average
would avoid a direct relationship between the individual processor's
sales management and growers' payments. Under the present system of
dividing future income, the beet grower shares to the extent of 50
or 60 percent in the marketing risk of the industry, whether it is
risk of lower price or risk of obtaining a higher price at too high
a merchandising cost. Conversely, he has the opportunity for increasing his return. Use of the national average return, either net
or gross, passes a large part of that risk to the processor--in whom
title to the physical commodity has resided since delivery of the beets.

Normally, one must be paid for assuming a risk. Under closely
competitive conditions, a beet processor will feel unable to guarantee
unconditionally the same scale of payments that he now promises condi-
tionally. Most business transactions do involve fixed prices, however,
and it is conceivable that beet growers and processors could reach
agreement on the value and cost of the shift in risk involved.

Any one of the national sugar price series mentioned above could
be used as a basis for sugar beet payments, with approximately the
same effect as explained for the use of national average gross returns
from beet sugar sales. Numerous variations in methods might be employed, each of which would give a slightly varying result.

Results of adjustments for individual factories or areas would
be differently affected insofar as their historical net return series
differed from the national-average returns. For example, if for a
given factory during the last 7 years, net return had declined 1 percent a year compared with the national average, adjustment of the
period as a whole (the average for the period) would still leave the
current net figure for the factory 4 percent below the national net
return figure. The local net would remain related to the national
average as at present. There was found, in fact, very little difference in the shape of historical series of data among areas or among
factories.

In general, the prices of sugar beets reflect area differences
in transportation costs of sugar from competing sugar sources. And
they seem to give clear evidence of rivalry among areas in a search
for the best markets.

These differences in competition that influence sugar beet returns by area cannot be altered by any change in method of computation. In addition to the regional differences, certain individual
plants exhibit levels of net returns quite clearly different from
the general run. Conditions permitting such differences may relate

either to unique production or market situations or to different merchandising policies on the part of factory management. In either case, they affect mostly the level of the series of data, not its shape.

Examination of the type of contract employed by sugar beet producer and processor in the Intermountain and West Coast sugar beet regions, and consideration of their economic effects make three points clear:

(1) Over the past three decades, no substitution of one of the national sugar price series as a basis of beet payments would have made a significant difference in beet prices.

(2) The processor and the grower have shared the marketing risks of the industry. If either the grower or the processor is to carry a greater part of the risk than he carries under the present agreement, he will expect to be paid for doing so. Any such change would be expected to appear as a change in the payment, or the scale of payments, for beets.

(3) Complete removal of the marketing risk from the shoulders of the grower would require an entirely different basis of payments. It would require a fixed price for beets of a given quality, determined before (and regardless of) the sale of the resulting sugar.

Whether or not avoidance of marketing risk through a fixed price would pay the grower could be determined only by the bargaining process. The outcome would normally depend on whether he or the processor was willing to carry the risk more cheaply. In brief, the grower can expect neither the assurance of a better scale of payments for beets by changing the method of computation, nor assurance of a greater profit by avoidance of a share in the marketing risk.

DETAILS OF POSSIBLE PRICING ALTERNATIVES

Under present contracting methods, when the grower and processor sign a contract for the coming season, the level of the year's payments is left to be determined by the net return that will be received from the sugar sold (1) from the one factory or (2) from a group of factories in one area.

Growers have objected to having the merchandising of sugar from a factory, or a group of factories, under the sole direction of the processors. The arrangement leaves the grower with a major interest in the efficiency of merchandising, but with no voice in the protection of that interest. Growers themselves have suggested possibly meeting the objection by shifting the basis of/payments to some national-average sugar price for the season, that would be independent of efficiency in the specific area.

Grower groups have advocated several alternative methods. The simplest and most direct way of making a shift to meet the objection would be to base adjustments on a regional or national-average net return for beet sugar during the season. In the following discussion the national average is used. It would require obtaining the ratio of local net to national net, then multiplying the national net by that ratio in order to obtain a derived net payment figure to which to apply the payment scale table currently in use. This derivation obviously could not be made from prices (net returns) for the season to be adjusted, or the correction would necessarily equal zero. It must be derived from some past period considered close enough to normal to give an acceptable relationship. A long period of years should give a very stable relationship that could change but slightly from year to year. A long period, however, might include wide changes in conditions and relationships and thus result in significant differences from current relationships.

The use of this method may be illustrated on the assumption that average price for the 7 preceding years would be used in determining prices in the current year. Obviously, a base period of any length could be selected.

The national average net beet sugar return that would be used in the 1955 season is $7.02. Its changes over the 5 preceding seasons are shown by the following 7-year averages, applicable to the adjustment of prices for sugar beets in the seasons 1949-50 through 1953-54.

7-year average national net return on beet sugar sales

Years	Net
1943-49	$5.89
1944-50	6.23
1945-51	6.60
1946-52	6.94
1947-53	6.94
1948-54	7.02

Each factory, or group, would likewise be able to establish in any year, by a few minutes' computations, its own average net return for the preceding 7 years, and the ratio of that average to the corresponding national average. Level of beet payments for the current season still would be unknown until net return nationally was computed for the season.

For all sugar beet growers combined, this 7-year average national net basis would have brought the same return as was actually received during these years, provided the same payment scales were used. But in locations where net return was rising less than the national average, growers would have benefited; where net was rising faster it would have held growers' payments to a lower figure than they actually have been. The benefit or the detriment would have been temporary. As the 7-year average was moved forward 1 year at a time, each year's divergence between local and national net would exert its share of influence on the succeeding year's ratio, so that continual adjustment of local net to national net would keep the two from drifting far apart.

As a second alternative basis of grower payments, three national series of sugar prices have been suggested. Throughout the period 1925-54, the 4 series, (1) raw sugar, (2) wholesale refined sugar, (3) retail refined sugar, and (4) the net return for sugar beets lay quite closely parallel to each other (figure 3). One of the periods of greatest divergence consisted of the 4 years during the war, 1942-45, when the 3 price series held almost precisely constant whereas net returns rose appreciably. By 1948, however, the 4 were in about the same relationship as in 1943. Thus, to have employed any 1 of the 3 sugar price series in place of net return could have been expected to have little short-term practical effect on the basis of payment. This assumes, of course, that a payment scale parallel to those now in operation would have been used.

In figure 3, the 3 price series are shown as ratios to net returns. Despite a very slight downward trend in retail prices, both the retail and wholesale series seem to have run very closely parallel to net returns. Trend of the raw-sugar price line does diverge slightly more from net returns. All 4 series are based on interrelated economic phenomena and, under free competition, cannot long differ greatly in movement except for differential developments in processing and marketing techniques.

In applying any 1 of the 3 price series as a basis of payments, various methods could be used. Any tendency of the long-term averages of the series to drift apart could be largely avoided by using averages for numerous short periods instead of 1 long one. Such lines also lessen irregular short-term movements that appear in the original data. A 7-year moving average has been used here for the same reasons and in the same way as illustrated for the adjustment to national net return for beet sugar.

Figure 4 represents 3 series of 7-year averages of annual ratios of sugar prices to net returns for beet sugar. This 7-year average base, applied first at the beginning of the 30-year period, then moved forward 1 year at a time, shows for the past 23 years a possible adjusted basis of payment (figure 5).

The suggested basis does not get entirely away from net return. It simply adjusts the local net return for beet sugar to a national average price for all sugar. Method of calculating the adjustment might be varied in several respects, but without very significant effect on the results.

The third alternative would base sugar beet payments entirely on the gross proceeds of beet sugar sales for the factory or area. It would treat merchandising costs like processing costs, in that

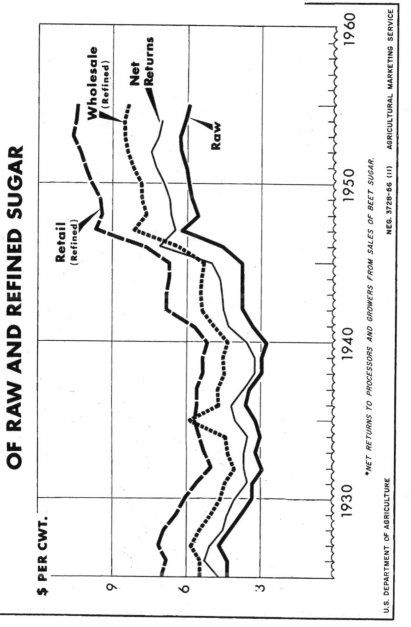

OF RAW AND REFINED SUGAR

$ PER CWT.

Retail
(Refined)

Wholesale
(Refined)

Net
Returns

Raw

1930   1940   1950   1960

*NET RETURNS TO PROCESSORS AND GROWERS FROM SALES OF BEET SUGAR.

U.S. DEPARTMENT OF AGRICULTURE   NEG. 3728-66 (II)   AGRICULTURAL MARKETING SERVICE

Figure 3

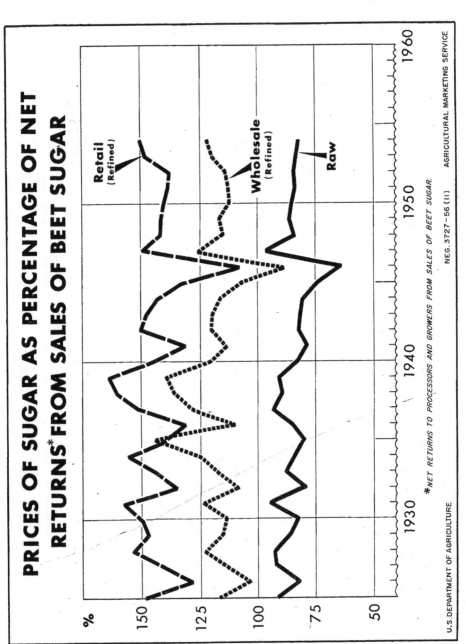

PRICES OF SUGAR AS PERCENTAGE OF NET RETURNS* FROM SALES OF BEET SUGAR

Retail
(Refined)

Wholesale
(Refined)

Raw

%
150
125
100
75
50

1930   1940   1950   1960

*NET RETURNS TO PROCESSORS AND GROWERS FROM SALES OF BEET SUGAR.

U.S. DEPARTMENT OF AGRICULTURE   NEG. 3727-56 (11)   AGRICULTURAL MARKETING SERVICE

Figure 4

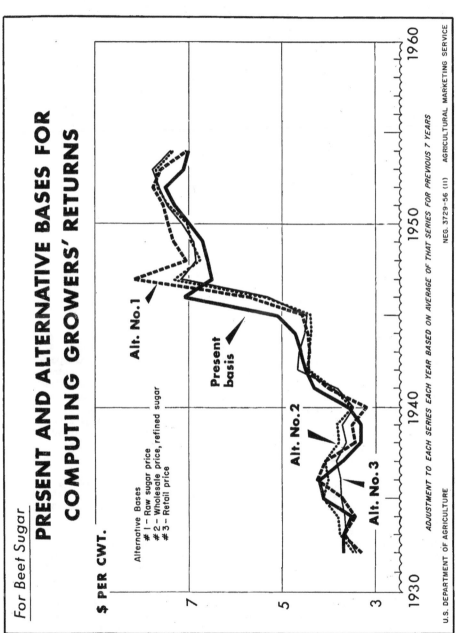

For Beet Sugar

PRESENT AND ALTERNATIVE BASES FOR COMPUTING GROWERS' RETURNS

$ PER CWT.

Alternative Bases
1 – Raw sugar price
2 – Wholesale price, refined sugar
3 – Retail price

Alt. No.1

Present
basis

Alt. No.2

Alt. No.3

1930   1940   1950   1960

7

5

3

U.S. DEPARTMENT OF AGRICULTURE   *ADJUSTMENT TO EACH SERIES EACH YEAR BASED ON AVERAGE OF THAT SERIES FOR PREVIOUS 7 YEARS*   NEG. 3729–56 (11)   AGRICULTURAL MARKETING SERVICE

Figure 5

they would not be deducted from returns before calculating a producer's payment as a share in returns. And the gross return would
represent the specific sugar sold by the beet sugar industry rather
than a United States average for all sugar.

Payment-scale tables used at present on a net-return basis could
be converted to a gross-return basis by applying to each net-return
bracket (line) the ratio of gross return to net return. The 7 years
for which data are available permit an approximate comparison of gross
and net returns for beet sugar. They show net returns equal to approximately 80 percent of gross returns, as follows:

Year	Percent
1948	79
1949	79
1950	80
1951	80
1952	80
1953	79
1954	79

A conversion of current sugar beet payment scales to a gross-
return scale on a national average basis can thus be made with good
approximation. It requires reading the figures in the net-return
table as gross returns and reducing the figures for beet prices
(growers' payments) to 80 percent of their present value.

The grower would still be left dependent on the processor's
ability to get a high total return for sugar sold, although his payments would no longer be affected by the processor's costs in obtaining high gross return. There would be a conflict of interest between
grower and processor in any situation where increased cost would
obtain higher return, but not enough higher to pay the extra cost.
If the higher gross return were obtained, the grower would gain and
the processor would lose, whereas if the lower gross were accepted
in order to obtain the maximum net, the processor would gain and
the grower would lose.

Merchandising activities are carried on, and costs incurred, to
obtain the best market possible. A marketing agent must be free to
direct merchandising activities and to finance his efforts without
penalty if he is to fulfill his responsibility to obtain the best
possible return for the product. Judgment is involved both as to
how much to spend and as to how to spend it. In an individual case
more than one policy may prove equally good. A high gross price at
high cost may yield the same net as a lower gross at low cost. High
transportation to distant points may bring a net return equal to con-
centrated sales effort closer to the point of production. Low merchandising expenditure can result in either a high or a disastrously
low level of net, and so, too, can high expenditure. Proper management of a sales department calls for high ability and continuous

study. Not only returns to the company but the amount that the company can pay for beets presently depends on these merchandising results.

It has appeared to some growers that net returns could be raised materially by improving merchandising efficiency and lowering merchandising cost. Those groups apparently appreciate the fact, however, that the matter is one in which arbitrary, uninformed, or unwise decisions can be economically ruinous. The ideal objective is optimum selling effort and cost, and no one is too sure in a given case just what is optimum. Obviously, this report has been designed to analyze some of the more pressing issues.

The sharing of marketing risks between grower and processor and the contingent returns to be assigned to each in compensation must finally be determined by a bargaining process to determine which one is willing to carry the marketing risks at lower cost.

BACKGROUND

The background for the development and the present status of the United States sugar industry is outlined briefly in the following pages. An understanding of this background is an essential to the solution of many of the sugar industry problems.

From early times, efforts have been made to exploit the sugar-producing possibilities of the United States, although sugar always has been an important import commodity. For nearly a century, the Government has recognized the need of tariff protection to foster the domestic sugar industry. It has maintained a continuous system of import duties or domestic subsidies to aid domestic producers. Production of sugar, first from mainland cane, then from both cane and beets, has grown through the years so that many agricultural communities now put great economic dependence on it.

During the years of agricultural distress in the early nineteen-thirties, a system of "agricultural adjustment" was developed, and sugar was included as a basic commodity. The Jones-Costigan amendment of the Agricultural Adjustment Act of 1934 established marketing quotas for sugar from the individual offshore supply areas, and for mainland cane sugar and mainland beet sugar. After the Act of 1934 was declared unconstitutional in 1936, the quota system which it had established was reaffirmed by a joint resolution of Congress in 1936, followed by the Sugar Act of 1937.

The 1935-39 average world production of sugar amounted to about 29 million tons a year, of which the United States mainland produced less than 2 million tons. The 1950-54 world production averaged over 38 million tons a year, and United States mainland production was then about 2,200,000. Annual consumption of sugar on the United

States mainland totaled about 6,700,000 tons in 1935-39 and 8,100,000 tons in 1950-54. In both years, this was between one-fifth and one-quarter of world production (table 4).

The Sugar Act was designed to supply the United States market with the amount of sugar that would be taken by consumers at "fair and reasonable prices." The "reasonable" price established was one that permitted sugarcane and sugar beet producers to compete economically with other farm enterprises in maintaining production to fill the mainland sugar quota. Since World War II, mainland production has supplied roughly a quarter of our sugar needs. In addition, two offshore United States sources (Hawaii and Puerto Rico) have supplied the mainland with about 90 percent as much sugar as is produced from mainland sources. Almost all the remainder has come from two foreign, but favored, areas, Cuba and the Philippine Islands. The official designation of these two countries as sources of import sugar results in part from a feeling of close relationship between them and the United States. The arrangement results in a significant betterment in the foreign trade balance of both Cuba and the Phillipines. Table 5 shows the composition of the United States sugar supply since 1935, its disposition, and consumption per capita.

Since 1933, the Government, under the Federal AAA and Sugar Act programs, has made payments to sugarcane and sugar beet growers in varying amounts by years, that at one point equalled two-thirds of the price of sugar beets paid to growers by the processors. During the last 8 years, these payments have remained under 25 percent of the sugar beet price, and in 1955 were around 20 percent. They have permitted a correspondingly lower price to consumers than otherwise would have been required to maintain this domestic production. The funds for such payments come from sugar processing taxes. This means that the subsidy is borne indirectly by consumers. Competition from foreign and offshore domestic sources has been held to a predetermined level by the quotas.

Until the 1954-55 season, the sharing of quotas among cane sugar refining companies and among beet sugar companies was left to the industry. On the 1955 crop, specific quotas in terms of tons of sugar that might be marketed were given for the first time since World War II to each beet sugar company by the Secretary of Agriculture, under authority of the Sugar Act and its amendments. Division of mainland production between cane and beet producers during these last 20 years has ranged, with exceptions, between three-fourths beet to one-fourth cane and four-fifths beet to one-fifth cane.

Cane sugar marketed on the United States mainland is distributed preponderantly from a relatively few points, whether ports of entry or areas of production, along the coasts. This situation has fostered a relatively simple distribution pattern and competitive relationships in the United States sugar market.

Table 4.—World sugar production, United States production, and United States sugar deliveries,1/ annual, 1935-1955

Year	World production			United States production 2/			United States deliveries	
	Total	Cane	Beet	Total	Cane	Beet	Total	Per capita
	1,000 tons	1,000 tons	1,000 tons	1,000 tons	1,000 tons	1,000 tons	1,000 tons	(Pounds 96°)
1935.....	26,093	15,097	10,996	1,650	382	1,268	6,634	104.26
1936.....	27,402	16,209	11,193	1,833	438	1,395	6,706	104.74
1937.....	29,423	17,070	12,353	1,832	459	1,373	6,671	103.57
1938.....	28,918	17,300	11,618	2,375	584	1,791	6,643	102.34
1939.....	30,842	18,139	12,703	2,262	506	1,756	6,868	104.95
1940.....	29,869	17,126	12,743	2,213	332	1,881	6,891	104.31
1941.....	27,110	17,690	9,420	2,008	416	1,592	8,069	120.97
1942.....	25,933	16,260	9,673	2,188	458	1,730	5,466	81.06
1943.....	25,246	16,503	8,743	1,497	497	1,000	6,335	92.65
1944.....	22,441	14,539	7,902	1,485	437	1,048	7,147	103.29
1945.....	20,803	14,227	6,576	1,749	475	1,274	6,041	86.34
1946.....	25,382	17,097	8,285	1,947	425	1,522	5,621	79.51
1947.....	27,791	18,806	8,985	2,216	377	1,839	7,448	103.35
1948.....	31,201	19,791	11,410	1,847	477	1,370	7,343	100.16
1949.....	32,001	20,346	11,655	2,091	521	1,570	7,580	101.62
1950 . :	36,182	21,477	14,705	2,576	564	2,012	8,279	109.17
1951.....	38,351	24,008	14,343	1,968	419	1,549	7,737	100.24
1952.....	36,200	23,366	12,834	2,110	605	1,505	8,104	103.22
1953.....	40,454	23,931	16,523	2,447	630	1,817	8,485	106.30
1954.....	40,542	24,945	15,597	2,653	610	2,043	8,207	101.06
1955 3/...	41,126	25,163	15,963	2,369	580	1,789	8,392	101.57

1/ Raw value. Crop years, beginning in year shown. 2/ United States mainland. 3/ Preliminary.

Source: The Sugar Situation, U. S. Dept. of Agr., AMS, pp. 2 and 23, March 12, 1956, also U. S. Dept. of Agr., CSS, Sugar Division.

Table 5.--Sugar, cane and beet: Stocks, production, trade, and supply available for consumption in continental United States, 1935-55

Year	Production 1/	Visible stocks beginning of period 1/ 2/	Receipts from-- Foreign sources 1/	Receipts from-- Territories 1/	Commercial exports and shipments 3/	Department of Agriculture net purchases for export	Domestic disappearance Military 4/	Domestic disappearance Civilian	Domestic disappearance Per capita consumption (refined) 5/
	1,000 tons	1,000 tons	1,000 tons	1,000 tons	1,000 tons	1,000 tons	1,000 tons	1,000 tons	Pounds
1935.....	1,583	2,178	2,763	1,815	132			6,622	95.7
1936.....	1,607	1,585	2,999	1,868	86			6,683	96.0
1937.....	1,821	1,490	3,280	1,883	93			6,651	95.1
1938.....	2,207	1,730	3,073	1,810	78			6,630	93.9
1939.....	2,320	2/2,305	2,975	1,872	153			6,859	99.4
1940.....	2,104	2/2,615	3,006	1,855	193	184	95	7,031	94.4
1941.....	2,090	2,356	3,997	1,852	91		424	7,960	102.8
1942.....	2,151	2,149	1,928	1,607	55	474		5,034	80.7
1943.....	1,531	2,138	3,431	1,510	18	730		5,623	79.7
1944.....	1,510	1,765	3,930	1,547	24	317	1,014	6,170	88.3
1945.....	1,666	1,227	3,226	1,647	34	175	6/1,094	5,045	72.9
1946.....	1,900	1,418	2,697	1,504	258	139	6/ 119	5,551	74.1
1947.....	2,160	1,452	4,217	1,812	232		6/ 114	7,357	94.2
1948.....	1,921	1,938	3,320	1,733	77		6/ 76	7,263	92.7
1949.....	2,114	1,496	3,809	1,893	44		58	7,451	94.5
1950.....	2,466	1,759	3,783	2,173	60		65	8,217	99.4
1951.....	2,042	1,839	3,725	1,918	82		127	7,552	92.5
1952.....	2,102	1,763	3,897	2,004	29		117	7,999	96.8
1953.....	2,375	1,621	3,881	2,249	32		97	8,358	96.5
1954.....	2,610	1,639	3,799	2,097	8/29		79	8,106	95.0
1955 7/..	2,386	1,931	4,029	2,155	8/45		74	8,385	95.8

1/ Data from Sugar Division, Commodity Stabilization Service. 2/ Beginning 1939 includes mainland cane stocks and beginning 1940 includes raws for processing held by importers other than refiners. 3/ Includes sugar used in the manufacture of other commodities. 1935-41 export data from U. S. Department of Commerce, Foreign Commerce and Navigation; 1942-53, quantities delivered for export as compiled by Sugar Division, Commodity Stabilization Service. 4/ Data based on allocation audits and records kept by the armed forces. 5/ Adjusted for changes in invisible stocks (estimated) held by manufacturers, wholesalers, and retailers. Population adjusted for under-enumeration. Civilian per capita consumption, 1941-55. 6/ Includes shipments for civilian relief feeding. 7/ Preliminary. 8/ Includes 9,000 tons for livestock feed in United States in 1954 and 19,000 tons in 1955.

Source: The Sugar Situation, USDA, March 1956.

A unique feature of our beet sugar production is its location at scattered points in the Lake States, on the Great Plains, and westward to the Pacific Coast. A further mark of distinction between the cane sugar and beet sugar industries on the United States mainland concerns the size of cane and beet growers. Cane growers average around 75 acres of cane per farm, and 85 farms per sugar mill. Beet growers average only 35 acres of beets per farm, and more than 300 farms per sugar factory.

The ratio between beet and cane sugar production is quite different for the United States from what it is for the world as a whole. In both 1935-39 and 1950-54, about 40 percent of world sugar production was beet sugar; the percentage dropped slightly, however, during the period. During the same 20-year period, a little less than three-quarters of the sugar produced on the United States mainland was beet sugar, whereas around four-fifths of our sugar consumption was cane sugar.

DEVELOPMENT OF BEET SUGAR PRODUCTION

Beet sugar production in the United States got an important start in the last quarter of the nineteenth century, reaching about 100,000 tons by 1900. By 1937, the industry produced $1\frac{1}{4}$ million tons of sugar a year from 9 million tons of beets. Since then, it has produced annually quantities varying from a million to 2 million tons, or roughly 4 to 7 percent of the world sugar supply. With a few years excepted, domestic beet sugar has supplied the United States mainland with about a fifth to a fourth of the sugar consumed.

As early as 1913, sugar beet production employed nearly 600,000 acres of land in the United States. Since 1937, acreage harvested has varied from 545,000 to 950,000, with a decrease of approximately 10 percent for the period as a whole. During the same 20-year period, production of beets has increased by about one-third. Yield of beets has increased around 40 percent, but the average sugar content of the beets has decreased slightly (from 16.4 percent in 1935-39 to 15.7 percent in 1950-54) (table 6).

The price of beets rose a little more than 100 percent during the 20 years 1936-55, but, because of increasing yield per acre, the amount the processor paid the grower for the beets from an average acre increased about 150 percent. With Government payments added, the increase was greater than 200 percent, or nearly as great as the increase in the national average farm receipts from marketings plus Government payments (table 7).

Mechanization has been carried a long way during the 20-year period, with consequent increased equipment costs, but with decreasing use of labor. Improved cultural practices have sometimes increased costs, sometimes decreased them, in varying situations. There

Table 6.--Sugar beet farms, beet acreage, yield per acre, and production,
United States, 1935-1955

| Year | Farms | Acreage | | Yield per acre 1/ | Production |
		Planted	Harvested		
	Number	1,000 acres	1,000 acres	Tons	1,000 tons
1935....	2/	810	763	10.4	7,908
1936....	2/	848	776	11.6	9,029
1937....	47,100	816	755	11.6	8,772
1938....	56,395	985	931	12.4	11,579
1939....	57,580	990	916	11.8	10,770
1940....	54,595	975	914	13.5	12,291
1941....	48,609	794	753	13.7	10,298
1942....	55,343	1,050	953	12.2	11,672
1943....	35,271	617	545	12.0	6,523
1944....	35,185	636	556	12.1	6,757
1945....	38,631	778	715	12.1	8,673
1946....	41,229	919	818	13.3	10,863
1947....	40,844	984	893	14.2	12,684
1948....	31,323	776	670	13.5	9,073
1949....	31,581	785	703	14.9	10,468
1950....	37,328	1,012	924	14.7	13,585
1951....	27,409	763	696	15.1	10,497
1952....	23,553	716	661	15.4	10,181
1953....	24,846	815	765	16.3	12,507
1954....	27,965	943	855	16.1	13,766
1955 3/.	24,960	802	748	16.5	12,238

1/ Harvested acre.
2/ Information not available.
3/ Preliminary.

Source: U. S. Dept. Agr., Commodity Stabilization Service, Sugar
Division, and Agricultural Marketing Service.

seems to be no good evidence that costs have risen more in sugar beet
production than in agriculture as a whole. Acreages of beets and size
of farms are both large in the Pacific Coast region, mechanization is
relatively easy, nearly all of the beet crop is irrigated, and on a
large proportion of the farms it is coordinated with other farm enterprises that use much of the same equipment and facilities. Cost of
beet production seems to have risen much less in the region during
the past 5 years than it has in the rest of the country.

Fragmentary data available suggest that, for the short period
1947-51, average cost of growing sugar beets for the country as a
whole rose 25 or 30 percent, varying geographically from around 45

Table 7.--Returns to growers for sugar beets, United States, 1935-1955

Crop year	Net returns per 100 pounds of sugar (Basis of payment 1/)	Payment to growers per ton of sugar beets purchased				
		Processor payments 2/	Sugar Act payments		CCC payments	Total
			Sugar 3/	Abandonment and deficiency payments		
	Dollars	Dollars	Dollars	Dollars	Dollars	Dollars
1935	4.05	5.76	1.20	---	---	6.96
1936	4.25	6❓	-	-	---	6❓
1937	3.68	5.27	1.86	0.10	---	7.23
1938	3.29	4.65	1.84	.06	---	6.55
1939	3.58	4.77	1.90	.09	---	6.76
1940	3.58	5.11	1.83	.06	---	7.00
1941	4.32	6.46	1.80	.04	---	8.30
1942	4.52	6.78	2.38	.18	---	9.34
1943	4.58	7.48	2.51	.18	---	11.54
1944	4.67	7.74	2.58	.19	1.36	11.51
1945	5.05	8.03	2.49	.18	2.87	13.37
1946	7.13	11.10	2.43	.15	2.15	12.82
1947	6.48 4/	10.60	2.44	.12	1.30 4/	13.65
1948	6.61	10.38	2.40	.10	---	14.44
1949	6.69	10.87	2.47	.16	---	12.94
1950	6.96	11.22	2.40	.07	---	14.44
1951	7.27	11.67	2.38	.08	---	13.41
1952	7.46	12.05	2.37	.08	---	13.70
1953	7.14	11.53	2.35	.06	---	14.13
1954 5/	7.14	11.10	2.32	.04	---	13.92
1955 5/	7.00	11.10	2.32	.10	---	13.52

1/ The net returns from beet sugar as defined in sugar beet purchase contracts. Does not include returns from byproducts. 2/ Basic payment. Includes growers' share in byproducts where purchase contract provides for such sharing, but excludes allowances for hauling, pitting, siloing, etc. 3/ Total payment. Breakdown between payments made for sugar and abandonment and deficiency not available. 4/ In addition, processors received an average of 47 cents per 100 pounds of sugar from CCC to compensate them for the difference between the actual net returns realized and the net returns required to return to growers the "price support" level for the 1947 crop. 5/ Estimated.
Source: U. S. Dept. Agr., Commodity Stabilization Service, Sugar Division.

percent in the East to perhaps 5 percent in some western areas. The areas where production has been increasing most rapidly, however, show a significantly improved ratio of gross return to production cost.

During the period 1937-54, the number of beet sugar factories in operation in the United States decreased from 87 to 69, while the amount of sugar they produced increased by 50 percent. Also, at the same time that the factories were decreasing in number and becoming bigger, in terms of beets processed and sugar made, the number of farms producing sugar beets decreased by 40 percent and average acreage of beets planted per farm nearly doubled. Net effect on total beet acreage was a decrease of somewhat more than 10 percent (table 8).

Changes in beet production had a clear geographical pattern. Increases in acreage occurred in the Red River Valley of North Dakota and Minnesota and in the Pacific Coast States. Sugar Reports of the Sugar Division, Commodity Stabilization Service, for September 1956 indicates the situation for approximately the period being examined, as follows:

"About one-fourth of the increased yield per acre during the 1949-54 period was due to shifts in planted acreage among the geographic regions.

"Although total acreage planted to beets in the United States during the 1952-54 period was only 4 percent smaller than during 1949-51 and 16 percent smaller than during 1938-40, acreage in the Eastern region was 33 and 56 percent smaller, respectively. On the other hand, planted acreage in the Far West was up 5 and 12 percent from 1949-51 and 1938-40, respectively, and in the Central region it was unchanged from 1949-51 but down 15 percent from 1938-40. Thus, it is obvious that the acreage planted to sugar beets has shifted westward since before the war.

"On the basis of elapsed time, shifts from 1949-51 to 1952-54 were sharper than from 1938-40. Sugar beet acreage in California, Washington, and Idaho in the Far Western Region was up in 1952-54 compared with both the 1938-40 and 1949-51 periods as a result of shifts from other Regions. Yields per acre in these States are high, and acreage abandonment in 1954 was only 4 percent. Both of these factors tend to lower production costs.

"Geographic shifts in beet sugar production also had a substantial effect on the sugar marketing situation. For instance, the excess of production over beet sugar deliveries in the beet-growing States of the Far West in 1954 was 513,000 tons as compared with 158,000 in 1951 and 480,000 in 1940, despite the increasing share of beet sugar to total sugar deliveries in that region from 41 percent in 1940 to 54 percent in 1951 and in 1954. The Central region, closer to the large beet sugar consuming area around Chicago, reduced its excess production over local use to 296,000 tons in 1954 and 278,000 tons in 1951 from 370,000 tons

Table 8.--Number of beet sugar factories, average production
per factory, number of farms, and acres of beets per farm,
United States, 1935-1955

Year	Factories	Average production 1/	Farms	Average acreage of beets 2/
	Number	1,000 bags	Number	Acres
1935.......	100	237	3/	3/
1936.......	98	266	3/	3/
1937.......	99	260	47,100	17.3
1938.......	100	337	56,395	17.5
1939.......	99	332	57,580	17.2
1940.......	97	365	54,595	17.9
1941.......	92	322	48,609	16.3
1942.......	89	362	55,343	19.0
1943.......	86	217	35,271	17.5
1944.......	85	232	35,185	18.1
1945.......	85	281	38,631	20.1
1946.......	85	345	41,229	22.3
1947.......	85	411	40,844	24.1
1948.......	83	296	31,323	24.8
1949.......	83	362	31,581	24.9
1950.......	81	465	37,328	27.1
1951.......	78	369	27,409	27.9
1952.......	75	378	23,553	30.4
1953.......	73	480	24,846	32.8
1954 4/....	73	512	27,965	33.7
1955 4/....	71		24,960	

1/ 100-pound bags refined.
2/ Planted.
3/ Information not available.
4/ Preliminary.

Source: U. S. Dept. Agr., Commodity Stabilization Service,
Sugar Division.

in 1940. In the Eastern region, 1940 sugar production was approximately one-half of beet sugar deliveries, but by 1951 and 1954 that
share had declined to about one-fifth. Thus, longer hauls and higher
transportation costs were incurred for increasing amounts of beet
sugar as production continued to decline in the East and to increase
in the West."

ECONOMICS OF THE INDUSTRY

The drift of sugar beet production westward apparently means that beets have become poorer competitors with other crops in the East and at the same time have become better competitors in the Far West. Many eastern beet growers appear to have been turning to other farm enterprises. At the same time, however, the average size of United States farms has been increasing with mechanization. Consequently a part of the decrease in number of farms growing beets in some areas, and some of the increase in acres of beets per farm undoubtedly represent this changing size of the individual farm business.

In general, throughout the domestic sugar industry there has been continual competition for a larger share in the sugar market. The mainland industry (cane and beet) has striven for a larger total marketing quota. Individual sugar processing companies frequently have stated their number-one problem as restricted marketing allotments. Both beet and cane growers as a whole have been quick to defend their acreages; that is, their shares in the total acreage contracted by the factory to which they sell their beets. But this inclination of the growers to prize their acreages has become severely weakened in some areas. For example, whereas acreages of beets per farm in California are large (around 100 acres) and increasing, some eastern factories are finding it necessary to pay bonuses to improve the competitive position of beets among available farm enterprises and thus maintain a processing volume that will permit factory operation on an economical level. As noted on page 28, acreage in the Eastern Region has decreased rapidly in the last 4 years.

With the geographical shift in production, there has come necessarily a reshaping or remapping of the movements of beet sugar from factory to consumer. During the earlier growth of the beet sugar industry the most favorable beet sugar market had developed in the region around the northern Midwest and Great Plains factories. Freight to that region was greatest from cane sugar sources on the periphery of the country; it was least from the beet sugar factories close by. As beet sugar production has moved westward, the product has continued to flow to the same general area (fig. 1 and table 9). This has required longer hauls, and consequently higher marketing costs, as defined in typical contracts between western beet growers and processors.

To bring beet sugar from the Pacific Coast to replace Intermountain or eastern sugar in the Midwest obviously costs about as much in freight as it does to bring competing cane sugar from West Coast refineries. Such increased freight costs do appear to have raised merchandising costs sharply for beet sugar from the Far West during the past three seasons. These facts indicate that insofar as West Coast beet sugar, rather than cane sugar, has taken over the share of the market given up by eastern beet sugar, it has been a triumph for production and processing efficiency over increasing marketing disadvantage.

Table 9.--Production and deliveries of beet sugar by processors, by State, 1954

State	Production 1/	Deliveries 2/
	1,000 tons	100-pound bags, refined equivalent
Arizona................:	--	167,994
Arkansas...............:	--	62,955
California.............:	4,319	7,374,572
Colorado...............:	1,654	966,040
Idaho..................:	1,569	301,066
Illinois...............:	36	6,508,590
Indiana................:	1	736,354
Iowa...................:	7	1,308,912
Kansas.................:	62	996,891
Kentucky...............:	--	1,000
Michigan...............:	771	2,520,444
Minnesota..............:	818	1,874,064
Missouri...............:	--	1,164,850
Montana................:	683	339,525
Nebraska...............:	786	1,378,737
Nevada.................:	--	22,508
New Mexico.............:	6	187,986
New York...............:	--	362,232
North Dakota...........:	418	334,376
Ohio...................:	247	547,915
Oklahoma...............:	--	435,416
Oregon.................:	389	866,153
Pennsylvania...........:	--	41,123
South Dakota...........:	75	377,931
Texas..................:	20	1,192,433
Utah...................:	534	534,999
Washington.............:	761	1,417,142
West Virginia..........:	--	4,442
Wisconsin..............:	135	1,576,639
Wyoming................:	475	141,538
Total...............:	13,766	33,744,827

1/ Preliminary.
2/ Distribution by primary distributors.

Source: U. S. Dept. Agr., Commodity Stabilization Service, Sugar Division.

Not only has production efficiency of beet growers increased, but also the West Coast beet sugar factories undoubtedly are able to attain relatively high efficiency and low processing cost because of the increasing acreage of beets contracted and the increased volume of beets processed in that region. There is a question, of course, how greatly a given factory can profitably increase its operations. Nevertheless, the universal attitude of beet sugar factory operators seems to be that additional marketing allotments, and hence higher rates of operation, would improve their economic position.

At the same time that expansion has been going on in the West, many factories in the Eastern Region have been faced with a choice between paying higher prices for beets to forestall the shift of beet acreage to other crops, on the one hand, and operating at lower volume and higher cost per ton, on the other hand. The heavy decreases in acreage in some areas indicate that the latter choice was made. A compromise decision appears, however, in those areas where bonuses are being paid to growers with large acreages. In this latter situation, the grower with physical conditions (of soil, terrain, labor supply, etc.) less suited to beet growing may have shifted to other crops, but some of the growers in better situations have increased their acreages and their efficiency of production, and also obtained a more attractive price for beets.

A certainty in all these varying situations is that the factory has to have sufficient beets for an efficient level of operation if it is to compete with other sources of sugar. Furthermore, the factory has but one economic use, the making of sugar. To continue in business and avoid the loss of its capital, it has to have the beets, and it has to pay a price necessary to get them.

CPSIA information can be obtained
at www.ICGtesting.com
Printed in the USA
BVHW050107061118
532207BV00024B/3546/P